Praise for *Juche: How to Live Well the North Korean Way**

'Rocket Man's little red book.'
President Donald Trump

'Every G8 nation has its own hardback wellness gifting book.
This book demands North Korea has a seat at the table.'
Pyongyang Literary Review of Books

'People ask, "What's the book that has
changed your life?" I tell them this.'
Priti Patel, UK Secretary of State

'I'm not a reader myself, but the Mrs chose it for
her book club and they absolutely lapped it up.'
Dominic Raab, UK Foreign Secretary

'On behalf of the 52%,
I'd like to raise a frothy pint
to Comrade Hyun-gi.'
Nigel Farage

'Why are we cutting down
the Amazon? So that books
like this can be printed.'
President Bolsonaro

'HOLY FUCK! I've gotta tell Elon about this.'
Joe Rogan

'No comment.'
Seth Rogen

'No comment.'
James Franco

---

* In case of any legal backlash, cyber-attack or assassination attempt, the reader should note that these quotes are a figment of the author's imagination, although the author would like to stress that any endorsements from the above sources would be gratefully received.

JUCHE

★

HOW TO LIVE WELL
THE NORTH KOREAN WAY

BANTAM PRESS

TRANSWORLD PUBLISHERS

Penguin Random House, One Embassy Gardens,
8 Viaduct Gardens, London SW11 7BW
www.penguin.co.uk

Transworld is part of the Penguin Random House group of companies
whose addresses can be found at global.penguinrandomhouse.com

Penguin
Random House
UK

First published in Great Britain in 2020 by Bantam Press
an imprint of Transworld Publishers

Copyright © Oliver Grant 2020

Oliver Grant has asserted his right under the Copyright, Designs and
Patents Act 1988 to be identified as the author of this work.

Photo credits: pages 12–13, 30–1, 60–1, 74–5, 90–1 © Alamy; pages 36, 38, 45, 56, 72, 125
© Shutterstock; pages 41, 46–7, 81, 102–3, 118–19 © Getty Images; author photo © Tara Rowse

A CIP catalogue record for this book
is available from the British Library.

ISBN 9781787634152

Typeset in FS Kim by Couper Street Type Co.
Printed and bound by Clays Ltd, Elcograf S.p.A.

Penguin Random House is committed to a sustainable
future for our business, our readers and our planet. This book
is made from Forest Stewardship Council® certified paper.

www.greenpenguin.co.uk

For Comrade An-dwu

Contents

Prologue

Dear Publisher,

Blessings from Pyongyang. If you are reading this then my work is done. My drone has mercifully evaded the cruel bullets of the imperialist wolves who stalk the shores of our peninsula and the wisdom of these pages has reached you in one piece. Blessings also that the battery did not give out over the Pacific, though I should not be surprised: North Korea produces the most durable and long-lasting batteries known to mankind.

My name is Comrade Hyun-gi. Born in 1941, I am one of the many unsung heroes of the DPRK (Democratic People's Republic of Korea). Blessed with health and armed with fortitude, I am most fortunate to have contributed to the socialist struggle and to have served as the Global Juche Ambassador under three generations of Glorious Kim rule.

North Korea is the envy of the world. Great Leader Kim Jong-un and his immortal forefathers Kim Jong-il and Kim Il-sung have taught us of your sinful ways. We know of your poisonous markets and corrupted societies, we know of your dirty capitalist leaders who neglect the wellbeing of their people in the blind pursuit of profit, and we know of your scheming efforts to crush the Juche revolution and bring about our ruin.

As the Global Juche Ambassador, the Great Leader bestowed upon me an almighty mission. I was tasked with travelling deep into the belly of enemy territory, to observe how the cogs of the capitalist machine work and, where possible, to try and spread the word of Juche. What I saw on that trip left me shaken to my core.

After presenting my findings to the Most Supreme General, he has subsequently reached out to the western world, inviting you to put down your faulty rockets and embrace our way of living. Each offering of peace and prosperity has been met with childish aggression by you and your imperialist cronies. Despite this, I cannot contain the tear of pity that falls from my heart when I think of you.

For I know the world you live in, I have seen the shortcomings of your society, and I know you are not yet alive to the joys of Juche.

For this I am sad a thousand times.

If your society refuses to listen to our Great Leader, then I hope you will listen to me. In sending out this drone, I hope the wisdom of these pages can reach your shores and transform your bodies and minds too. By publishing the word of Juche we are advancing the great revolution so that one day we can march together, as comrades in arms, towards the socialist bliss that awaits us.

Comrade Hyun-gi,
Pyongyang

Juche 주체, *'self-reliance'*
Pronunciation: *'joo-chay'*
Ju translated: *Master*
Che translated: *Material or thing*

Meaning

Translated, Juche means 'self-reliance'. It asks us to dig within ourselves for the resources to fulfil our potential and achieve the great socialist revolution.

The Juche philosophy forms the unbreakable foundation of our most mighty culture; it is the bed we lie on and the goal we work towards. By realizing the power within each comrade, the Fatherland can be free from the headlock of capitalist forces and exist as a self-sufficient socialist nation.

Conceived for the people, Juche states that only man, through backbreaking work, soul-nourishing study and boundless courage, is capable of driving progress. It teaches us that man must work together, as the masses, to bring about change.

But man can only work together if there is a Supreme Leader who represents the masses. The Supreme Leader is essential for our safety and success: without him we would be unable to survive. The masses are at the centre of the revolution, and at the centre of that centre is the Supreme Leader.

This is the heartbeat of Juche.

History

Juche was conceived by the Immortal Father, Kim Il-sung. The Great Leader was an expert on all the philosophies of the world; he spent four years meticulously digesting the abridged works of Marx and Lenin, and he advised the great socialist leaders of the age – Joseph Stalin and Chairman Mao. He also spoke to Fidel Castro twice on the telephone and sent an encouraging telegram to the office of Harold Wilson.

It was in the 1950s, as socialist nations began to tremble at the foul capitalist winds that blew from the west, that General Kim Il-sung entered his period of intense study. To ensure the prosperity of Korea and its comrades, he needed to create a way of life that was superior to our socialist allies', one that would further our great revolution and provide contraception against imperialist forces.

After months of scholarly meditation, forgoing meals, afternoon naps and deep-tissue massages, the Great Leader emerged from his study tired and a bit peckish but overcome with joy that he had created a philosophy that would inspire the masses, defend the country from capitalism, and establish Korea as a united, independent and prosperous nation.

Juche was born.

Practice

The Great and Sunny Leader gave us Juche, and the fruits of his philosophy provide for all the children of the revolution, giving us hope, safety and dignity on our blissfully isolated peninsula.

In the Fearless Father's most original and earth-quaking manifesto, he declared that Juche would ensure ideological autonomy ('Chaju' 자주), economic self-sufficiency ('Charip' 자립) and military independence ('Chawi' 자위).

Combined, these elements provide the DPRK with an iron spine of heavy machinery and limbs of the most advanced technology, allowing us to walk free from the booby traps of international politics to stand alone, and stand taller than every other nation.

This is the great gift of Juche.

– KIM IL-SUNG, REASSURING
FACTORY WORKERS,
PYONGYANG, 1963

WORK

In capitalist societies, where morals are depraved and sin is as rife as rice, money reigns supreme. The western world claims to be 'the land of the free' but in truth it is the land of the slave. Man is a slave to the dollar. And no matter how hard he fights it, his work and worth will always be measured against it.

This tugs at my pity strings.

In the DPRK, our work is driven by a higher purpose. Together, we comrades work under the direction of the Wise and Benevolent Leader to bring about the self-sufficient glory of Juche. By working towards an ideology, not the dollar, we are liberated from the evils of capitalism and are free to achieve our independence.

The western world has no such ideology; instead its workers are driven by the stench of stocks and shares. Thus they are denied the joys of Juche and meaningful work.

In this chapter I will explain the merits of Juche industry and how our nation's working conditions have become the envy of the world.

The Art of Balance

'*We must live to work, not work to live.*'

– KIM JONG-UN, ADDRESSING HIS BASKETBALL COACH, AGED SEVEN

One of the greatest battles in western culture is the quest to find the work–life balance. Attempts at achieving this have led corporations to spew millions of dirty dollars on bogus ideas such as flexi-working, gong therapy sessions, and something called 'annual leave'. There is a simpler way.

In North Korea we live by the simple philosophy that Work = Life and Life = Work.

As such, we live in perfect harmony.

Work (Life)   **Life (Work)**

- Our intelligence has intercepted reports that western employers are plotting to impose a four-day working week on their employees.

- These agents of sloth must be removed swiftly and violently.

- Once these idle culprits have been arrested and disposed of, a seven-day working week should be introduced with immediate effect.

Work Where You Sleep

The most common complaint of the western worker was their daily commute to work. Due to extortionate rates of rent and a medieval railway infrastructure, the commute is an arduous march that bookends each day. It is a sinful pilgrimage and a daily reminder of western man's servitude to the dollar.

'The fisherman must sleep at sea, the miner must sleep in his mine, the butcher must sleep in the abattoir.'

– KIM IL-SUNG, ADDRESS TO THE NATION, 1956

Studies from Pyongyang Secondary School show that a stressful commute increases feelings of helplessness and despair within the working man.

Workers of the DPRK are not subject to such traumatic daily migrations. Instead, we are instructed to sleep under our desks. By doing so, the workplace becomes a second home and we comrades are able to enjoy longer working hours.

- All comrades must bring a pillow and small blanket to work with them. These can be stored under the desk, which can then be transformed into a makeshift bed.

- Soft toys, eye masks and earplugs are allowed subject to official review by a comrade's line manager.

- Our comrades at Huawei have adopted this approach and reported a marked improvement in their output and the wellbeing of their staff.

The Gender Pay Gap

After lengthy 'chinwags' with western human resources (HR) officials, I was left warm with rage to learn of the existence of the gender pay gap – a deep crevasse of prejudice which runs through western society, discriminating against workers on the basis of a chromosome.

*'What's in a chromosome?
Am I right?'*

– KIM JONG-IL, INTERNATIONAL WOMEN'S DAY, 1994

This bias is cruel and wrong. It prevents women from achieving their true potential and contributing to the revolution.

Workers of the DPRK have never suffered such mistreatment, and never will. Our Just and Egalitarian General ensures that all comrades, men and women, are paid the same – 4,800 won a month (roughly $4). A most generous gift from our Great and Well-Endowed Leader.

Diversity Hinders Production

'*Too many cooks spoil my soup.*'

– KIM JONG-UN, ADDRESSING HIS PERSONAL CHEFS, AGED FOUR

After my daring mission in the western world, I concluded that the place had sleepwalked into an unruly mess. For too long its cultural commentators have encouraged citizens to love themselves for who they are, peddling the lie that there is no such thing as the ideal comrade, that comrades of all shapes, sizes, attitudes and hairstyles are worthy servants to the cause. This is not the case, and it poses grave problems for the world of work.

If the workplace becomes infected with a non-homogeneous workforce, employers are forced to appease each comrade's individual wishes and demands – their fashion sense, their dietary requirements, even their preferred computer operating system. The list goes on, and the workplace soon becomes a political minefield similar to that which runs along the 38th parallel.

Juche has taught the DPRK to tighten its cultural borders, protecting its people from the disease of individualism. This pays dividends in the workplace: by ensuring that each worker is a replica of the other, true progress can be achieved.

HR Tip

- All HR departments should introduce mandatory background checks on any potential employees.

- If HR managers notice any signs of difference, they must alert security who will prevail on the individual to conform, on pain of indefinite detention or deportation.

Maternity Leave Should Not Mean Eternity Leave

The birth of a new comrade is a most sacred event.

After interviewing several maternity nurses, I was horrified to discover that western women are banished from the workplace after having a child. These women often then struggle to return to the workplace after this prolonged period of absence.

On hearing this, my heart bled one hundred milli-litres.

'The umbilical cord of socialism feeds every child of the revolution.'

– KIM JONG-IL, *DIARIES VOL. II, 1976-82*

Juche values the birth of a child above all else. For this reason, the DPRK invites mothers to bring the baby straight from the hospital to the workplace. This way the mother is able to resume her revolutionary work immediately and the child can quickly become acclimatized to the workplace environment.

The factory becomes their nursery, heavy machinery their lullaby, annual reports their bedtime story. The workplace is a second womb.

Man is Measured on Merit Alone

'It is not who you know but how hard you are willing to work.'

– KIM IL-SUNG, *ON THE NATURE OF PROGRESSION*, 1963

During my reconnaissance mission around the western wasteland, I applied for several jobs and internships. After multiple rejections and misdiagnoses by CV doctors, I realized that corruption is rife in western employment. Opportunities are handed to those with the largest contacts book, not the largest work ethic.

Jobs are exchanged for holiday homes. Promotions are swapped for improved exam results. The sons and daughters of bouncers are shown to the front of the queue.

Juche teaches us that progression can only be achieved through honest hard work. Nepotism is a disease which must be treated with the following antibiotics:

- Shady social networks such as 'LinkedIn' and 'Bebo' should be banned.

- 'Work socials' including dinners, lunches and corporate entertainment should also be prohibited.

- Only the Great Leader can decide who is promoted, based on a comrade's productivity.

- No one is able to influence the Great Leader's decision because we always keep a respectful distance from him.

Invest in Younger Generations

Socialism grows from the root upwards. Juche asks us to put our faith in the young generations, giving them responsibility from an early age.

The west is wicked and distrustful of its youth; it patronizes them by withholding responsibility and challenges until later life. In doing so, it invites the younger generation to turn their faces from their elders

In the DPRK, every child is in full-time labour by the age of six. Typical roles include operating sewing machines, tilling rice fields and small-scale nuclear testing. By introducing our children to the rituals of revolutionary work at such an age they are irradiated with the revolutionary spirit and are masters of their own destiny.

'*No child is too young to join the revolution.*'

– KIM IL-SUNG, VISITING A MATERNITY WARD IN PYONGYANG, 1957

Fun Fact

At the age of fourteen, a DPRK worker has the same level of professional experience as a thirty-year-old western adult. This is the secret of our success.

The Forest is a Free but Inefficient Market

'A free market is held captive by the evil forces of capitalism.'

– KIM JONG-IL, *MEDITATIONS FROM PYONGYANG*, 1994

The economy is a forest. In the western economy, trees and plants compete with one another to reach the top of the canopy and absorb the sun's energy. But so much of that energy is wasted in growing the trunk to help them reach the top.

In the socialist economy, our Great and Tall Leader instructs all the trees to remain at ground level.

That way they can absorb the same amount of energy from the sun but not waste it on growing their trunks.

This is the secret to an efficient economy.

- The western world can easily correct its markets by nationalizing every industry.

- Until recently, General Kim Jong-un was in regular contact with Comrade Corbyn and Comrade Sanders on how best to do this, advising them on their economic policies.

'If capitalism is so great, why does it need to be rescued by Communism every fifteen years?'

– KIM JONG-IL, DEBATING
WITH POTATO FARMERS, 1997

While our cultures are poles apart – and ours vastly superior – I was quietly encouraged to see the small similarities in our ways of life. These fleeting parallels gave me hope that the roots of socialism could one day take hold in the hostile soil of capitalism and perhaps grow into a society that is worthy of calling itself our ally.

Sadly, I now realize that this is the most distant of dreams . . .

Maovember

As autumn turned to winter in the west, I observed the ubiquitous sprouting of hairs above the lip sills

'*Come, shave your heads in remembrance of me.*'

– KIM JONG-IL, OPENING A BEAUTY SALON
IN PYONGYANG, 1999

of young men. What sorcery was this? The roots of the Fourth Reich? I investigated this fascist phenomenon in more detail and discovered that for one month a year, western men ask people to give them money in return for styling themselves on Adolf Hitler.

North Korea does not tolerate such political blasphemy. Instead, it demands that all male comrades adopt a Maoist hairstyle for the month of November, using a simple rice bowl to coif their natural fibres in remembrance of our great and fallen socialist ally.

Half Marathons

'*The revolution is a marathon, which must be a sprint.*'

– KIM JONG-UN, HALF-TIME TEAM TALK TO THE PYONGYANG UNDER-11 ATHLETICS TEAM, 2011

Born from our ancient games on Mount Paektu, the marathon marks the greatest feat of athletic endeavour. Our Immortal Leaders continue to set new world records for its completion:

- Kim Il-sung, 1971: 1hr 55min
- Kim Jong-il, 1997: 1hr 49min
- Kim Jong-un, 2019: 1hr 45min

When strolling through Central Park one day, I was left dazed and confused by the amount of praise being shovelled upon those who had only completed half this feat. Why is this a cause for celebration?

The North Korean marathon is the original and most challenging course. It is not for the faint-hearted. There are no prizes for those who stop halfway.

No athlete of the DPRK would ever think to celebrate completing half a task. Any cowards caught walking or celebrating prematurely are immediately rounded up and sent back to the beginning where they are forced to start the challenge again.

Reduce Your Carbon Footprint

While the planet heads ever closer to Armageddon, nations continue to bicker and squabble over half a degree. The Mature and Moral High Grounded Leader has decreed that the DPRK should withdraw

'Self-sufficiency? Girl, get back on your boat. We're way ahead of you on this one.'

– KIM JONG-UN, VOICE NOTE TO GRETA THUNBERG, 2019

from these childish quarrels and combat the climate crisis on its own terms.

After years of intense study and research, the Great General published instructions on how comrades can enhance the wellbeing of the planet, and, in turn, themselves.

- Comrades should live off a strict rice-based diet.

- The only form of transport is public transport. Personal cars, motorbikes and Segways are reserved for the Dear Leader and his family's busy working schedule.

- Anyone caught using a private motorized vehicle shall be sentenced to three months' work in the Faecal Energy Fields.

- Harmful-to-the-environment luxuries such as central heating and gas stoves shall be prohibited in all homes.

- Pesticides and fertilizer shall be replaced with natural alternatives (human waste).

- A no-fly zone is to be implemented over Korea. Comrades who wish to take a holiday should explore the beaches, mountains and cultural riches that are contained within the borders of the DPRK.

The Milky Way

Soya, almonds, rice, oats, even goats ... As I perused the coffee houses of the western world, it was plain for me to see that they are addicted to milking anything with or without a pulse. In some cases, they even milk pulses.

'Gladly we suckle from the teat of the state.'

– KIM JONG-IL, VISITING A DAIRY FARM, 1999

North Korea spares its cattle and crops this liquidating fate by instructing comrades only to drink what the state provides them with.

For generations, the DPRK has nourished its children with breast milk expressed by its most loyal comrades. Female comrades, whose families have demonstrated unwavering devotion and energy towards the Dear Leader and the Juche philosophy, are asked to donate their breast milk to the DPRK's Dairy Farm, where it is powdered, packaged and distributed to kindergartens across the country.

Known as 'white spirit' (새하얀 영혼), this milk contains the elixir of revolutionary life, allowing all comrades to cling to the bosom of the state and ingest the finest spirit of socialism.

Meal Prep

A growing phenomenon in the west is the term 'meal prep'. Citizens spend a whole day cooking large quantities of food, then dividing it into plastic boxes, taking a photo of them and sharing it on the internet, before freezing the boxes for the week ahead. This process is sold as being therapeutic, but in fact it prevents an individual from being present in the moment.

Too much forward planning steals tomorrow and takes away today.

> *'There is something liberating about not knowing where your next meal is coming from.'*
>
> **– KIM IL-SUNG, SPEAKING OUTSIDE A FOOD BANK, 1968**

In North Korea we are groomed to be present at all times and 100 per cent focused in the moment. Our highly efficient rationing programme encourages us to think only about the meal we have in front of us, not one in seven days' time.

Like, Share, Subscribe

'*Every revolutionary action is shared with, and liked by, the Great Leader.*'

– KIM JONG-UN, TWEET TO THE NATION, 2018

Western scientists have stumbled across a neuro logical malfunction in the brains of their citizens. Studies show that when a 'friend' shares or approves their online actions, the brain leaks great gallons of dopamine. This malfunction has given way to an online epidemic, where citizens spend every waking hour on their phones, seeking out love and valid-ation from their online 'friends'.

The comrades of North Korea do not waste their precious time with this mindless activity. We have grown up learning to love ourselves, safe in the knowledge that the Great Leader monitors our every movement. If we conduct ourselves in line with Party principles, then we will receive his un-conditional and boundless love.

Comrade Hyun-gi
16 mins

Comrade Chun-ku: Just volunteered to sample some uranium for The Great Leader's new arsenal. This stuff is STRONG. #LivingMyBestLife #CantFeelMyLegs #Blessed

👍❤️ Your post was liked by Kim Jong-un and 200k others

👍 Like   💬 Comment

Fashion

Each year western 'fashionistas' gather in Paris, Milan, New York and London to parade their ridiculous designs up and down the catwalk of capitalism. These crafty crooks then spend the remainder of the year bullying citizens into buying these ludicrous garments. The pressure to keep up with the latest fashion leads to mass anxiety and hysteria within the western population.

'Khaki is the new camo, Comrades.'

– KIM JONG-IL, PYONGYANG FASHION WEEK, 1994

The DPRK does not inflict such trauma on its comrades. In the early 1990s it introduced a mandatory and homogeneous fashion policy for the masses, which is still in effect today. All comrades of the DPRK are instructed to wear straight-cut military-chic uniforms. These are timeless in design, allowing all comrades – young and old – to be united in appearance and prepared for military action at the drop of a helmet.

'Zero cases of SARS.
No disease can infiltrate
the fortress that is the
socialist mindset.'

– DR KIM JONG-IL,
ADDRESSING THE WHO,
MARCH 2003

HEALTH

Juche is built on the health and strength of its revolutionary workers. The success of the revolution can only come about if our bodies and minds are fit for physical and ideological work.

While the Gentle and Attentive General tends to our every need, his endless meetings with Party members and international comrades and his strict basketball practice regime mean he cannot personally cure our every ailment and injury.

For this reason, the Kind and Compassionate Leader published a ground-breaking medical journal, providing us with wisdom and remedies for our conditions. Armed with these state-of-the-art medical techniques, we are no longer reliant on quacks and junior nurses to heal us. We have the tools to heal ourselves.

My research trip to the western world has shown me that your health services are nothing more than private cash cows, which politicians and drug addicts milk until the udders run dry.

I hope the findings in this chapter can provide you with the same revolutionary balms and ointments as they have done for us, restoring our souls to the peak of Mount Paektu health.

Sleep

While the revolution never truly sleeps, it is crucial for comrades to rest well. A good night's sleep is paramount for maintaining a happy and healthy mind. Failure to do so results in poor workplace performance, increased levels of stress and fewer revolutionary dreams.

The western workforce is made up of insomniac zombies. Late-night restaurants, excessive alcohol

'I sleep with one eye open, so you can sleep with both eyes closed.'

– KIM JONG-UN, ADDRESSING HIS INNER CIRCLE, 2017

intake and 'binge watching' mindless TV shows into the early hours of the morning leave westerners with great black satchels under their eyes.

To combat this, our Most Soothing Leader devised a foolproof way to ensure that all comrades get eight hours of sleep every day:

- From 11 p.m. onwards, a nationwide curfew wlll be brought into immediate effect.

- All electricity, media and transport is prohibited until 7 a.m. the following day.

- All comrades must remain under house arrest during this time.

- Any comrade caught violating the state curfew will be sentenced to a lifetime of sleep.

Diet

'Hunger is the soul's yearning
for the revolution.'

**– KIM JONG-IL, VISITING A FARMING VILLAGE
DURING THE GREAT FAMINE, 1998**

Gluttony is the deadliest of sins. Through gross indulgence, western citizens are eating themselves into an early mass grave.

On my travels to the capitalist continents, I watched in horror as they polluted their bodies with food twice, sometimes as many as three times, a day.

The DPRK ensures that all its citizens are fed and healthy. In the 1990s, when the headlock of international trade tightened around the neck of our innocent peninsula, our Slender Leader devised a highly effective rationing programme that was so successful it is still in use today. The plan left us with a streamlined workforce that was able to slip free from the chokehold of sanctions and live independently off the riches of Korean produce.

Our Abstemious and Mindful Leader is the living embodiment of this practice. He sets a worthy example to us all.

Kim Jong-il's highly effective rationing programme

- Families of the DPRK are to be given one bowl of rice a day, to be shared between family members.

- The act of sharing and sacrifice sets a good example to younger revolutionary comrades.

- Standard plate and cutlery size is to be reduced by 40 per cent – this maintains the illusion of a larger meal size while limiting a comrade's calorie intake.

- A reduction in quantity and muting of flavour in food has multiple benefits, including aiding digestion, reducing instances of IBS, and eradicating the 'food coma' which is known to hinder early-afternoon productivity in the workplace.

Exercise

Regular exercise is essential for maintaining a healthy happy glow. The western world is made up of lazy landlords and bedridden bankers, with 80 per cent of citizens failing to exercise on a regular basis. This leads to severe health problems later in life such as heart conditions, arthritis and extreme chubbiness. This was highlighted recently when our Most Athletic Leader was unable to stand toe to toe with Donald Trump, such was the extent of Mr Trump's belly.

For the 20 per cent of westerners who do exercise regularly, nearly all of them are members of something called 'the gym' – a crafty capitalist construction that uses body shaming and false advertising to bully downtrodden individuals into extortionate fixed-term contracts.

Since the birth of our Great Nation, the DPRK has provided all comrades with regular opportunities to socialize and exercise free of charge, the most popular of which are the daily parades led by the heads of the military.

- Parades happen every day between 3 and 4 p.m.

- Comrades gather in their town or village where they receive a motivational speech from the head of the military.

- The marching technique uses the body's full range of muscles – complete extensions of the legs, arms and neck in brisk repeated steps – allowing for a full-body workout.

Dry January

> '*I spent forty days and forty nights in Walmart without food or drink. Not once did I wilt to the sins of my surroundings.*'
>
> – KIM JONG-UN, *DREAMS FROM MY FOREFATHERS*, 2012

Each new year, after months of gluttony – spawned by the commodification of a bogus religion – western citizens become increasingly health conscious and choose to enter into a period of abstinence.

Those who undertake this vow of abstinence become suddenly righteous, using any social or professional engagement to lecture those nearby on the benefits of their reformed lifestyle. Phrases such as 'I'm sleeping so much better', 'My productivity has tripled' and 'My sperm count is up' are commonplace in the western world throughout the month of January.

Come the first day of February, these crusaders of hypocrisy revert to their old habits with a vengeance.

Health

In North Korea, we demonstrate our respect for the Great Leader by taking a vow of capitalist chastity *throughout* the calendar year. Abstinence makes the mind grow stronger. With this power we can repel the temptations of the western world.

'The greatest kind of love is tough-love.'

– KIM JONG-UN,
IN CONVERSATION WITH THE
WESTERN JOURNALIST AND
NOVELIST MATT HAIG, 2015

MENTAL HEALTH

Because the Juche philosophy is driven by ideological work, the upkeep of a comrade's mental well-being is essential for achieving the revolution.

Nothing is more contagious than an idea. For this reason, the DPRK ensures that all comrades' minds are armed against counter-revolutionary thoughts and remain open and receptive to ideas issued by the Party.

In the western world they have turned mental health into a get-rich-quick scheme. Thousands of celebrities, posing as experts, exploit the anxieties and fragilities of their fellow citizens for their own financial gain. These mongers of doom feed off the people's insecurities, selling them books, apps and podcasts which are loaded with made-up remedies. They make money out of sadness.

In this chapter I will share with you how our Wise and Compassionate Leader has protected us from these mindful mercenaries, and ensured that our mental wellbeing is as lush as the Pyongyang cherry blossom in spring.

Seasonal Affective Disorder (SAD)

'It is always sunny in Pyongyang.'

– KIM IL-SUNG, LECTURING THE DPRK METEOROLOGICAL SOCIETY, 1981

Like the DPRK, the western world is blessed to exist in the northern hemisphere, meaning its inhabitants are able to enjoy the variety of the seasons. To my horror, I discovered that westerners were not appreciative of nature's lush spectrum. When autumn turned to winter they scurried to their doctors, begging them for pills and other illegitimate remedies to cure their seasonal glumness.

Such ingratitude appalled me.

SAD has been eradicated in the DPRK because it is always sunny in Pyongyang. The Omnipresent

Leader shines down on us comrades at all times, even in the depths of winter when the days are as short as our life expectancy.

The only way in which to combat Seasonal Affective Disorder (SAD)

- Comrades should carry a picture of the Eternal Sunny Leader with them at all times, If comrades begin to feel negative thoughts, they should contemplate the picture of our Kind and Generous Leader for ten seconds. This will banish any signs of depression and leave the individual feeling light and happy.

Mindfulness

The mind can be a torrid place. For some it is a raging tempest, for others an eternal sunrise. Great Sunny Leader Kim Il-sung was blessed with a most cheerful head and instructed that all children of the revolution reproduce his naturally high levels of serotonin.

'My scythe hit the baked earth again and again and again. I felt no pain, only motion and rhythm. Wow, I thought, look how much land I have tilled!'

– KIM JONG-UN, APPEARING ON *KIM'S HAPPY PLACE PODCAST*, 2015

In the western world, one in three adults are plagued with depression. Their gloomy faces are riddled with sadness, so they turn to alcohol and drugs as a way to fix it. As their healthcare system continues to fail them, their governments have sold them something called 'mindfulness' – a new form of brainwashing which paralyses the individual into doing nothing for minutes and sometimes hours on end.

Studies from the Pyongyang Department of Neuroscience and Animal Experimentation reveal that this technique is nothing more than bogus witchcraft. 'Mindfulness' only hinders production and progress, while increasing the sense of worthlessness within the individual. Last month it published a revolutionary paper which set out effective ways to blow away the dark clouds of depression.

Mindfulness = **Manual labour**

- Studies show that repetitive tasks such as lifting, sewing and digging release serotonin in the brain.

- These activities also increase the self-worth and sense of productivity within the individual.

- Labour-intensive tasks should be carried out during all hours of the working day, and extra sessions encouraged if a comrade is struck down with counter-revolutionary thoughts.

- Any contemplation outside of the above activities should be restricted to musing on the fortune of having been born in the DPRK under a dynasty as benevolent and nourishing as ours.

Weaving

'*Each comrade's struggle is a thread in the great tapestry of socialism.*'

– KIM JONG-IL, DELIVERING THE EULOGY OF KIM IL-SUNG, 1994

Weaving is an ancient tradition of North Korea, dating back to the year 4000 BK (Before Kim). Our ancestors' nimble fingers joined the fibres of the earth to clothe and strengthen those who walked upon it. Legend has it that the weavers of Mount Paektu could keep going for months on end, uninterrupted, combining the sacred strands of our homeland to tell the story of how our great and prosperous nation came to be.

While I was pleased to see that our ancient ritual had taken hold in the western world, I was saddened to see how it had been hijacked by bourgeois internet princesses who sell weaving as an escape from the cause. These 'vloggers' instruct citizens to use their time to create items such as hats, gloves, tea-cosies and dog-jackets which serve no revolutionary purpose whatsoever.

Colouring-in

Studies show that colouring-in alleviates stress and reconnects adults with their inner creativity. While colouring-in has proved to be hugely popular in the western world, I was disheartened to see them wasting their energy on swirling patterns, mindless slogans, dot-to-dots and other such pointless pursuits.

In the DPRK, comrades are encouraged to colour in scenes of our illustrious history. By doing so, the individual is able to see the revolution in technicolour detail – restoring their hearts and minds to the Party principles.

'The revolution will be broadcast in HD technicolour.'

– KIM JONG-IL, SPEAKING AT THE
PYONGYANG BIENNALE, 2009

Western colouring-in

North Korean colouring-in

Therapy

Over the course of my daring reconnaissance mission, I discovered that almost every western hostage underwent regular therapy and counselling sessions. Probing further, I learned that these poor souls paid vast sums of money for someone to

'The examined life is not worth living.'

– KIM IL-SUNG, *MEDITATIONS FROM THE AUTUMN OF MY MIND*, 1983 sit and listen to them as they reclined on a studded leather chaise longue and poured out all their petty worries and woes.

When I asked them why they had to do this, they replied that it was because they felt they had no one else to turn to. Tears began to swim in the basins of my eyes . . .

I felt blessed that no such service is necessary in the DPRK, for every house in North Korea is fitted with a therapeutic bug. This miraculous piece of technology ensures that the Great and Compassionate Leader is listening to us every second of the day.

'There is only one true 'ism' – Communism.'

– KIM JONG-IL, OPENING
THE NATIONAL GALLERY
IN PYONGYANG, 2001

ENTERTAINMENT

Entertainment falls into two categories – high (하이아트) and low (낮은 예술).

High entertainment seeks to expand and challenge the mind of the audience. It is noble in its ambition, striving to enhance cultural and philosophical knowledge. This form of entertainment appeals to the highest sensibilities of human nature and forms the foundation of the DPRK's cultural output.

Low entertainment appeals to mankind's most basic instincts: sex, laughter, fear and more sex. This mindless content serves no revolutionary purpose. It has no ambition. This form of entertainment is the staple diet for citizens of the west. Greedily, they fill their eyes and ears with it.

In my travels to that torrid place, I discovered that the western media industry is nothing more than a prosthetic limb of the capitalist regime. Disguising low entertainment as 'high art', it appeals to the audience's most primal dispositions, using fake news and false ideals to lure in viewers before taking their wallets and souls hostage. It is a wolf in lamb's uniform.

The DPRK state media is guided by the Juche philosophy, creating entertainment of the highest order to celebrate the trials and tribulations of the revolution. This avant-garde approach unites the nation and guides us towards the new dawn of socialism.

Ted's Talks

Who is Ted? After being recommended his talks by nearly everyone I encountered in the west, I decided to sit down one evening to watch some of Ted's talks on YouTube. Hours turned to days, and days into weeks. When I emerged from this wormhole, I

*'I think it's fair to say,
I speak for everyone.'*

– KIM IL-SUNG, ADDRESS TO THE NATION, 1948

realized that none of the talks were delivered by Ted himself. I began to suspect that this 'Ted' may not exist ...

Our Dear Leader would never hoodwink his comrades like this. Every day, our Dear Leader gives an impassioned and informed talk to the nation, inspiring us with his boundless knowledge and intellectual prowess. His speeches inform us of all the ground-breaking work we comrades are doing and how rapidly the revolution is advancing.

He is the fountain of all knowledge. Gladly, we sup from it.

The K Factor

'*Although you have won, Korea is the real winner tonight.*'

– KIM JONG-IL, CONGRATULATING COMRADE MIN-KI ON WINNING *THE K FACTOR*, 2006

As well as being on the lookout for international spies and reasons to test our nuclear arsenal, North Korea is always looking to discover new domestic talent. To increase the search effort, Kim Jong-il created *The K Factor* – a television show inviting the people of North Korea to appear before him and showcase their artistic talent. The winner of *The K Factor* was then rocket-launched on to the international stage, shining as a beacon of Korean talent for the rest of the world to admire.

Like all good ideas, as soon as they are proved to be a success they are pirated by western television studios. One night, as I flicked through the channels in my Holiday Inn, I came across one counterfeit version, the imaginatively named *The X Factor*.

After enduring the show from the initial rounds through to the judges' houses and then on to the live shows, I felt offended – not by the exposed chest hair, bleached teeth and surgically altered faces on display, but by learning that I had to pay in order to vote for who I thought the winner was. What kind of democracy is this? At the end of my stay, my phone bill came to £213.56. Explaining this to the Party accountant made me very toasty under the collar.

Our Great Leader would never ask us to part with our hard-earned money to express an opinion. Instead, he chooses the winner of *The K Factor* on our behalf. We are always delighted with his choice!

How To Fail

As I rode the subway from one Juche convention to another, I noticed how many people were listening to a show called *How To Fail*. Intrigued, I began to eavesdrop on this weekly programme.

As far as I can make out, the show is hosted by an extremely successful and high-achieving woman

'*Failure is what separates the comrades from the counterfeits.*'

– KIM IL-SUNG, *MAO AND ME*, 1967

who wants to instruct people on how to fail better. I immediately sent this podcast back to our laboratory in Pyongyang for further inspection.

After extensive tests were carried out on the podcast and its audience, our experts concluded that the western world celebrates failure as a way of excusing their lack of productivity and success. This gives way to a 'victim culture' where citizens begin to display dangerous levels of self-pity, self-examination and self-sabotage.

North Korea would never encourage or instruct its comrades to fail. Instead, each morning we wake up to the national radio giving us clear and inspiring messages on how we can succeed in fulfilling our potential, fuel the fires of socialism and avoid placing our marching feet into capitalist traps.

Rom Coms

The most effective way to rouse the masses and cement their passion for the Party is to target where they are weakest – the heart.

In the early 1980s, the DPRK's Film and Cinematic Union created a new genre of film – a style so revolutionary and avant-garde that it will change the face of cinema for millennia to come.

'*Yes, many capitalists were hurt in the making of this film.*'

– KIM JONG-IL, SPEAKING AT THE PREMIERE OF *KIM'S JUST NOT THAT INTO YOU*, PYONGYANG INTERNATIONAL FILM FESTIVAL, 1998

Romantic Communist movies such as *Lovers in the Mine*, *Tractor Tank*, *Tractor Tank 2*, *Kim Kong* and *Kim Kong Strikes Back* became blockbuster hits, inspiring comrades across the globe to take up arms and join the struggle for socialism.

I am pleased to see these kinds of films slowly infiltrating the western bloodstream. My particular favourites are *Enemy at the Gates* and *Goodbye Lenin*.

Some western DVD sellers are classifying the following as 'Rom Coms', despite not showing any revolutionary characteristics:

- *When Harry Met Sally*
- *Love Actually*
- *The Holiday*
- *Ten Things I Hate About You*
- *Pretty Woman*

None of these films adhere to the DPRK's criteria of a Rom Com. They should be rebranded as 'soppy chuckle films'.

True Crime

Thanks to the pigs of Hollywood and their merciless truffle hunt for content, the western world has lost control of law and order. Their fetish for criminal activity has gone beyond the point of return, leaving its citizens in grave danger.

'Crimes against the state will
be punished – not televised.'

– KIM JONG-IL, AT THE OPENING OF A FAECAL
ENERGY FIELD IN PALBONG PROVINCE, 2004

During my travels behind enemy lines, it became
apparent to me that if a western citizen commits a
crime, partakes in a fraudulent scheme or tries to
foment mass civil unrest, they will be rewarded with
a ten-part television series or podcast. What blasphemy is this? The carrot and stick method doesn't
work if you only give people carrots.

'True Crime' is the fastest-growing sector of the
western media industry. Since the release of popular shows such as *Making a Murderer, The Jinx* and
Serial, crime rates in the western world have almost
quadrupled.

North Korea prioritizes the safety and welfare of
its citizens above all else. It would never look to
encourage or reward treasonous behaviour. Our
Great Nation prides itself on rounding up its dissi-
dents and detaining them indefinitely, not turning
them into overnight celebrity criminals.

State Media

'One Mission. One Nation.
One Voice.'

– KIM IL-SUNG, FIRST RADIO BROADCAST, 1953

After a long day ambassading Juche around the western world, I would retire to my room, eager to unwind with a film or slice of TV.

If I were to list the menu of choices put before me, I would be here until next year. Each evening I would try to pick something to watch, but by the time I had chosen what to watch, the birds were singing and it was already tomorrow.

I was not alone in this experience. After speaking to many western prisoners, they described a similar problem, with many couples confessing that they often spent more time debating what to watch than actually watching anything.

Every second of every day, western media companies are trying to seduce the eyes, ears and wallets of their citizens. They bombard their population with options, just as they bombarded our peninsula with bombs. Like their bombs, they left their targets paralysed. In this case, with indecision.

The DPRK vows never to inflict such trauma on its comrades. In a most generous and considerate act, Kim Il-sung launched the state media, offering us comrades one channel with all the information and entertainment we could ever need.

Typical state media timetable

07:00 – National Anthem / rousing ballads
07:30 – Dear Leader's Address to the Nation
08:00 – *Good Morning Pyongyang* with Comrade Myung-won
10:00 – *The Juche Show* feat. Comrade Sun-hye
13:00 – Lunchtime Nuclear Testing – Live!
14:00 – *Border Watch* with Comrade Dae-yung
17:00 – Cook Along with Kim-chi
18:00 – *The K Factor*
20:00 – Rom Com
22:00 – Kim's Bedtime Story

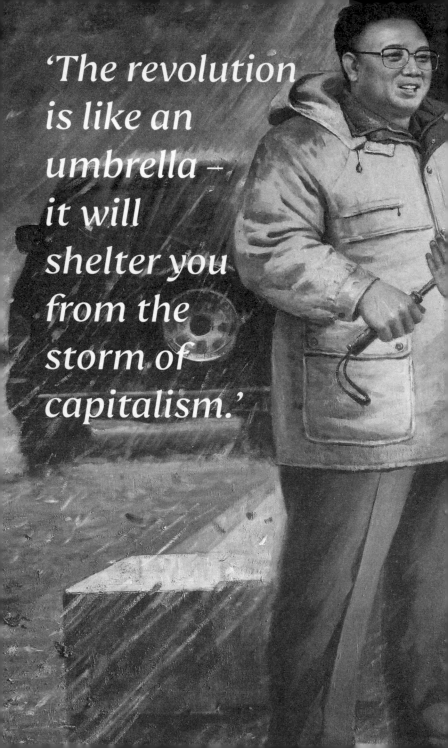

'The revolution is like an umbrella – it will shelter you from the storm of capitalism.'

– KIM JONG-IL,
VISITING A HOMELESS
SHELTER, 1978

THE
HOME

Homeowners of the western world use their dwellings as oversized trophy cabinets, filling them with pointless and expensive goods in order to show off to their neighbours, and from time to time the plumber.

Their narcissistic pursuit of perfection, through conservatories, power showers and new curtains, leads them nowhere – except deeper into the pockets of Mrs B&Q and Mr Ikea.

The homes of North Korea reflect the humility and respect of their occupants. They do not waste their time and energy on creating a show-home, instead they strip back their homes to the bare essentials, saving their flair and flourishes for revolutionary work.

Rent

'No man is a peninsula.'
– KIM IL-SUNG, *LETTERS TO A HERMIT KINGDOM*, 1980

In the western world, 60 per cent of the population spend over half their monthly salary on rent. This vast financial sacrifice is the price exacted by greedy capitalist landlords, who prioritize their wallets over the welfare of their tenants. These covetous tycoons seize great swathes of public land, before selling it back to the public at vast expense.

In its all-encompassing munificence, the DPRK has always provided homes for us comrades free of charge. In the 1960s, when the revolution was burning on all cylinders, the Party built thousands of state-of-the-art homes across the nation, providing families with a safe place to live.

While the western citizen pays a fortune to live in high-rise cabins with faulty heating systems, asbestos poisoning and dangerous levels of damp, they are also deprived of any sense of community. The

DPRK values community and comradery above all else and is keen to foster it in every home. For this reason they make sure three, sometimes four families live in the same room.

Pets

'Stop all the clocks, cut off the telephone,

Prevent the dog from barking with the bones of US soldiers.'

– KIM JONG-IL, FROM *THE COLLECTED POETRY OF KIM JONG-IL*, 1998

There is a saying in the west that goes 'dog is a man's best friend'. During my travels, I learned that many western citizens live by this mantra. The dog is undoubtedly a loyal and playful companion, and a welcome addition to any family unit. But after staying with these pet-owning families, the true extent of their obsession was revealed to me: they feed them extravagant meals, groom them on a weekly basis, provide them with medical care, brush their teeth, clip their nails, and escort them on daily private walking tours of the national parks.

They are blinded by their affection for these canine comrades.

Westerners would do well to remember that the pet is first and foremost a member of the military forces and a key weapon in a country's arsenal. The dog should be feared and respected in equal measure, not pampered like a princess.

House Plants

On the rare occasions I was welcomed into a westerner's home, I was amazed not only by how much they paid for these high-rise cubby holes but by how many plants their abodes contained. Cacti, succulents, shrubs and vines filled every inch of their living quarters. I couldn't help but think, if these people want to be surrounded by plants, why don't they just live outside?

In North Korea, the Kind and Considerate Leader is awake to nature's power and restorative qualities. Because of this, he kindly slashed the housing budget, encouraging more comrades to sleep out-side in makeshift dwellings so that they might reconnect themselves to the beauty of the natural world.

> '*Communism is the strongest and most natural of weeds; once it takes root, it is impossible to dislodge.*'
>
> **KIM JONO IL, ADDRESSING THE QUEEN AT THE CHELSEA FLOWER SHOW, 2003**

Neighbours

Nothing is more disruptive to the family home than disrespectful neighbours. Often on my travels I was kept awake late into the night by the sound of bick-ering through the walls. The root of this midnight quarrelling lay in a lack of respect for their fellow citizens: forgetting to take the bins out, failing to hand over post, not clearing up after one's pet, or blaring music into the early hours of the morning. These late-night rows left my host deprived of sleep and unable to work well the next day.

'*Denounce thy neighbour, as you would like to be denounced.*'

– KIM JONG-UN, SPEAKING AT A VILLAGE FETE, 2017

The DPRK has taken effective measures to ensure that no neighbour should become a barrier to revolutionary work. If a neighbour is caught committing small acts of vandalism or not seen to be conducting themselves in line with Party behavioural standards, comrades are encouraged to denounce them to their local informant immediately.

Denouncement Line: +850 421 880 990

- State your name, address and revolutionary number.

- Wait until you are connected to a denouncement officer.

- State the name, address and revolutionary number of the comrade you wish to denounce.

- State reason for denouncement (optional).

Interior Design

'*The home should display the inner workings of the revolution.*'

– KIM JONG-UN, PYONGYANG DESIGN WEEK, 2015

During my expedition to the western front, I stayed in many homes, with many affluent hosts, but I was disturbed to see what dishevelled and impoverished taste they had when it came to interior design: distressed mirrors, peeling paint, exposed brick walls, creaking floorboards, empty bottles used as lamps, factory pallets turned into makeshift tables, and mattresses simply placed on the floor as a bed. Such things, I was told, were the height of fashion.

We Koreans are proud people and proud home dwellers. We see our homes as an extension of ourselves. As such they are designed to reflect our austere love for the revolution and the Great Leader.

'I grew up with nothing and wanted for nothing for I had the Party's loving embrace.'

– KIM IL-SUNG,
MEDITATIONS FROM THE
AUTUMN OF MY MIND VOL. II, 1987

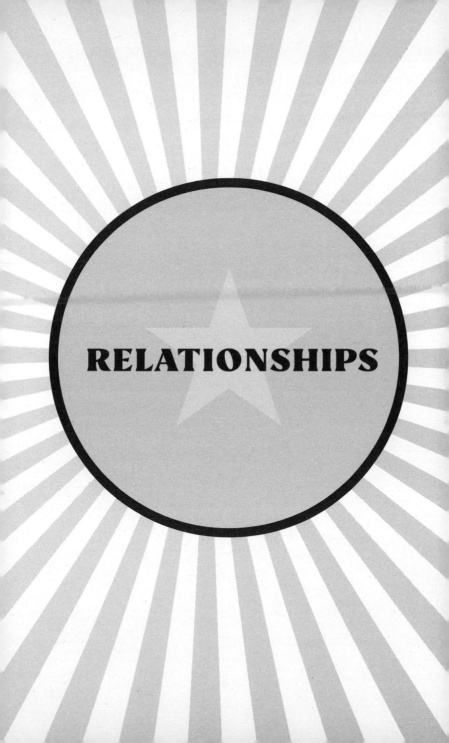

RELATIONSHIPS

Relationships are a science. They are the atomic bonds that bind comrades together and, in turn, unite us in the revolution. The stronger these bonds are, the mightier the nation is.

Western science has not progressed far enough to come to understand this. They still see relationships as an emotional commodity, a casual experience that can be exchanged or terminated at will. As such, their society is made up of floating atoms, alone and afraid, unable to come together for the common cause.

The people of North Korea set an example to the rest of the world. The love our Dear Leader shows to us comrades is replicated in the love and trust we display for each other. United, we form an impregnable structure that cannot be broken.

In this chapter I will reveal the tricks and tips on how to strengthen bonds between people, both inside and outside the family. By following these simple steps, your countries will discover how they too can come together and join the socialist march to freedom.

Dating Apps

'Harry Truman and I are proof that opposites do not attract.'

– KIM IL-SUNG, FATHERLAND LIBERATION WAR MUSEUM, 1953

Western citizens spend hundreds of wasted hours and dollars on finding a mate. Through mindless questions and 'small talk' they hope to stumble across the perfect match. This long and arduous march to find a partner is fraught with disappointment, rejection and heartbreak.

In North Korea, comrades are drawn to each other not because of whether they prefer dogs to cats, or think pineapple is acceptable on pizza, but because of their shared passion for the Party ideology and the teachings of Juche.

In recent times, westerners have turned to digital applications to help alleviate their loneliness, but the questions they ask and the answers they give reveal nothing about ideological compatibility.

Western dating app	North Korean dating app
Pet peeves Adults on scooters	*I wish to denounce* Capitalist landlords
Together we could Watch Louis Theroux documentaries	*United we aim to* March towards socialist bliss
The key to my heart is David Attenborough	*My love is bound to* The Great Leader
Where to find me at the party? In the kitchen	*Where to find me at the parade?* Front left, marching in brisk unison

Sex

'This is the fallopian tube
of the revolution.'

– KIM JONG-IL, UNVEILING A NEW MOTORWAY,
PYONGYANG, 2006

The carnal communion of comrades is a most sacred event. The joining of socialist flesh to create new revolutionary life is the river that supports Juche.

I find it hard to speak of the debauchery I was exposed to in the western world. Across the Pacific, sex is nothing but a commodity used to undermine women and tease open the wallets of morally unhinged pigs. I was alarmed to discover western children growing up with a most unhealthy view of sex, believing homosexuality, interracial copulation and carnal embrace outside the barbed-wire fence of marriage to be acceptable acts. They are not.

Thankfully, our Most Brave and Selfless Leader devoted many hours to the subject of sex, not just theoretically but practically exploring its intricacies on our behalf so that we comrades could develop a healthy attitude towards it. In his illuminating manifesto *When Two Become One to Make Three,* he provides clear instruction on how we can lead happy and healthy sex lives.

- Sex is prohibited outside of marriage and should only be undertaken for the practical purpose of creating new revolutionary comrades.

- Sex is a practical activity not a pleasurable one. Comrades need only be aware of the missionary position. Any attempt to explore adventurous techniques, including oral and clitoral stimulation, should be immediately reported to the authorities.

- Interracial sex is forbidden. Anyone caught diluting the Korean bloodline should be severely reprimanded. Punishment for repeat offenders to include chemical sterilization.

- Pornography is banned from the DPRK. All pornographic material should be handed over to the authorities, who will then pass the publications in question on to the Dear Leader for him to peruse and officially disapprove of.

Long-distance Relationships

When my mission came to an end and I was summoned back to Pyongyang, I noticed how many people were crying at the airport as they waved goodbye to their loved ones. These were not tears of joy. They were tears of sorrow at the prospect of being apart from those they held dear.

I felt my hand reach for a tissue . . .

'Presence makes the heart grow stronger.'

– KIM IL-SUNG, LETTER TO HIS SECOND WIFE KIM SONG-AE, 1987

The DPRK would never inflict such unnecessary heartbreak on its citizens. Through the introduction of an armed border and an extensive no-fly zone, comrades are liberated from the torment of long-distance relationships. They live safe in the knowledge that they will never be apart from their soul mate.

Absent Fathers

'What can I say, I have strong swimmers!'

– KIM JONG-IL, TAKING A PATERNITY TEST, 2003

According to reports, one in four children in the western world grow up in a fatherless household. With no male role models to look up to, a crisis of masculinity is sweeping its way through the western province. The lack of a father can lead to severe problems later in life such as an inability to shave, not knowing how to carve a chicken, and not learning how to accept you are in the wrong even when you're not.

No household in the DPRK is without a father, because the Supreme Leader is a father to us all. He shows us the ways of the world and we follow his example.

Difficult Teenagers

The road from childhood to adulthood is a rocky and untarmacked one, full of potholes and booby traps. One false step or wrong turn and teenagers can quickly find themselves down a dead end of debauchery and despair. This must be avoided at all costs. It is why this stage of life is crucial for the development of revolutionary attitudes.

It is very common for western teenagers to display the following troublesome tendencies:

• Apathy towards politics
• Overt lack of respect for their elders
• Obsession with the opposite sex
• Prioritizing sleep over work
• Monosyllabic chanting
• Violent mood swings

- Rebellious inclinations
- Increased levels of masturbation

The DPRK has created a foolproof way of ironing out such counter-revolutionary characteristics and relieving families of their pesky cubs during this difficult time.

All teenage comrades must undergo a five-year period of compulsory military service. Through severe discipline, prolonged absence from family members and constant exposure to the might of the DPRK's army, these comrades return to their family units as fully reformed disciples of the revolution. Any resisters are sent on educational expeditions into the country's interior that can last anything up to twenty years.

'We must kindle the flames of youth, so that the fire of revolution burns bright.'

– KIM JONG-IL, SPEAKING AT PYONGYANG SECONDARY SCHOOL PRIZE-GIVING CEREMONY, 2001

Sibling Rivalry

'Although we come from the same womb, there is only one winner.'

– KIM JONG-UN, DELIVERING THE BEST MAN'S
SPEECH AT KIM JONG-NAM'S WEDDING, AGED TEN

Not all families get along. Brothers and sisters can find themselves at war with one another. It has been that way since the beginning of time (Cain and Abel), and it continues to be this way today (the Williams sisters, the Gallagher brothers, Ed and David Miliband).

Western parenting gurus have come up with bogus techniques to try to quell such rivalry; they've tried celebrating siblings' differences, encouraging sharing and increasing inheritance tax – but none of these measures can halt the natural struggle for power between womb-mates. There is only one solution.

Kim Jong-nam was the eldest son of Kim Jong-il, and the elder half-brother to Kim Jong-un. Kim Jong-nam was not only a traitor to the DPRK, working as a spy for the CIA, he was also a thorn in the Great Leader's side, constantly trying to usurp his birthright and refusing to allow Kim Jong-un to sit in the front of the car.

On 13 February 2017, Kim Jong-nam was killed by nerve agent in Kuala Lumpur airport. It is said that Kim Jong-un was very sad to hear of his half-brother's passing. Kim Jong-un had no involvement with his death.

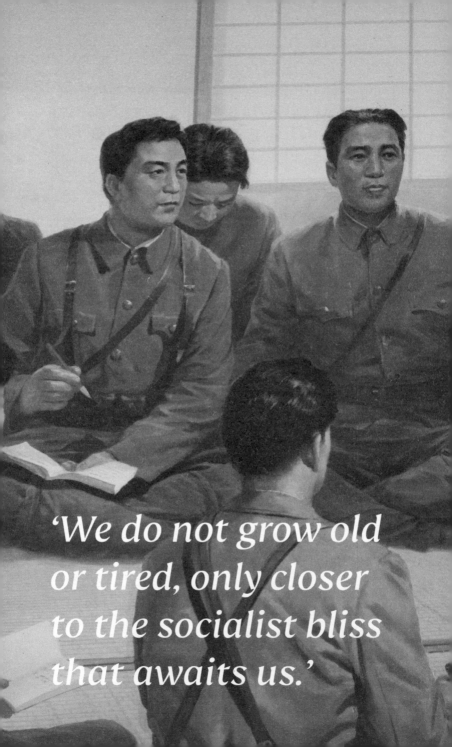

'We do not grow old
or tired, only closer
to the socialist bliss
that awaits us.'

– KIM IL-SUNG, LECTURING
HIS BATTALION, PYONGYANG
MILITARY BASE CAMP, 1997

AGEING

In the western world, society's gaze is fixed upon its youth in an unhealthy way. They spoil their youngest members, providing them with childcare and Kinder Buenos, and the opportunity to appear on *Junior Masterchef* and *Junior Apprentice*. And to think they call *us* the nanny state!

While the DPRK is respectful and encouraging of its young comrades, we are enlightened to the wisdom of our elders. Juche is built on a foundation of respect for our most elderly members. These comrades have walked furthest down the path of the revolution; as such their bodies and minds are full of revolutionary knowledge. By treating our elders with the compassion and dignity they deserve, they are able to pass on their knowledge from one generation to the next.

In this chapter I will teach you how to protect, provide for and learn from your elders. By reaching out across the gap of generations, one is able to seize the crop of knowledge and harvest the fruits of wisdom.

Retirement

The Juche philosophy instructs us to revere our elderly comrades, so I was appalled to see what disrespect the western world shows its own. When western workers enter their seventh decade – just as they are reaching the mastery of their profession – the state forces them to retire, granting them the freedom to pursue their own idle interests. Once retired, they are made out to be burdensome leeches on society, draining it of time, money and resources.

Juche forbids us from treating our elderly comrades with such disdain. Instead, it promises to protect

'Do not fell that tree, for there is sap in the old trunk yet . . .'

– KIM JONG-IL, ADDRESSING PATIENTS IN AN INTENSIVE CARE UNIT, PYONGYANG CENTRAL HOSPITAL, 2002

them from idleness and keep them employed until the day of their death, whenever that may be. This way, our elderly comrades are kept at the forefront of the revolution and can vigorously pass on their wisdom to the next generation of eager revolutionaries.

Winter Fuel Allowance

As the nights grew long and the temperature dropped in the western world, their newspapers became awash with righteous rants about 'the winter fuel allowance'. This is a bogus policy which panders to elderly citizens' idle and bourgeois claims of being unable to keep warm during the winter months.

> '*Come, warm your hands at the forge of socialism.*'
>
> – KIM JONG-IL, VISITING A MOUNTAIN HOSPICE, 2006

Not to my surprise, the west's wilted-spinach governments succumb to these pathetic pleas. This drains the state of its power reserves and permits these greedy layabouts to live in a home-sauna for up to five months of the year. This has serious knock-on effects for the rest of the country.

The DPRK does not bow to such petty qualms. Our elderly comrades are kept warm by keeping close to the fires of revolution. Their work and constant contribution to the struggle stirs their lions and warms their cockerels.

Pensions

As I travelled to and fro across the capitalist continents, the word 'pension' kept following me around like the CIA's private investigators.

Keen to learn more, I discovered that pensions are an obsession in the western world. People shovel great heaps of their income into these pots, hoping that one day they will turn into a magic money tree in whose shade they can sit for the remainder of their days.

While this sounds like a most fine and dandy plan, it is a wholly selfish act.

'There is no need for a rainy-day fund, for it never rains in North Korea!'

– KIM IL-SUNG, *HOME ECONOMICS VOL. XII*, 1977

The DPRK instructs that no comrade should hoard a pension for themselves. Anyone caught stockpiling financial reserves is to be immediately reported to the authorities, their assets given over to the state, and a fixed term of labour in the Faecal Energy Fields carried out.

Euthanasia

'*I put the mercy back into killing.*'

– KIM IL-SUNG, SPEAKING AT THE BIOLOGICAL WEAPONS CONVENTION, 1972

As the world continues to become overrun with 'OAPs', the western world is intent on finding new legal ways to kill them off.

The decision to end a family member's life prematurely is notoriously difficult, not to mention financially and emotionally crippling for those having to take such a decision.

The crafty capitalist care homes of Switzerland charge families extortionate rates to dispose of their loved ones. Despite the thieving nature of this scheme, families still travel thousands of miles and pay thousands of dollars for the service.

The DPRK acknowledges how emotionally taxing such a journey can be, and for that reason it relieves comrades of this duty. The DPRK decides at what point a comrade's life should come to an end.

It does so quickly and quietly, without warning, without complaint.

Cruises

After several meetings with the Western Board of Tourism, I discovered that a popular leisure activity for the elderly was to go on a cruise. These are ships of the living dead, floating mortuaries, which transport the ill and the deranged around the world, showing them sites and scenery that will be forgotten moments later.

The DPRK values a comrade's leisure time, but weeks at sea is a very inefficient use of that time, especially when it could be otherwise spent contributing to the cause.

For this reason, the DPRK has arranged unstaffed river cruises up the Taedong river. Elderly comrades can come aboard and marvel at the wonders of North Korea – the Nangnim Mountains, Mount Paektu, the Olympic Stadium and the Juche tower – even as they crew the vessel, attend to its maintenance and prepare their own food. This unsurpassable tour lasts exactly eight hours, allowing elderly comrades to resume their revolutionary work early the next day.

From glorious birth to glorious death in selfless service of the Great Nation – long live Juche!

'Why sail the high seas when you can sail on the winds of socialism?'

– KIM JONG-UN, BRIEFING THE DEPARTMENT OF TOURISM AND TORTURE, 2016

Epilogue

And so, dear comrades, I hope with all my heart that you will look up from these pages and see the world with fresh eyes. If my travels have taught me one thing, it is that we are never too old to change our ways.

On this earth, we comrades are blessed with the freedom to choose our way of life, to invest in an ideology and to believe in a leader who will protect and preserve us for centuries to come. The words in this book are a reminder of the choices we have before us, as well as an invitation to put down the past and join our great revolution.

Writing this book has been a deeply troubling but rewarding exercise. While I take no pleasure in shining a light on the darkness of your lives, I hope these chapters can provide comfort in the knowledge that there is another way, a better way – the Juche way.

Take a moment to stop. Listen to the rhythm of your heart. That is the marching beat of socialism – it lives inside every one of us. Lift up your eyes. If you look beyond the capitalist smog that pollutes your soul, you will see the flaming tower of Juche, burning bright beneath the peak of Mount Paektu. This, comrade, is where you will find us, with open arms, ready to march with you into the dawn of a new day.

Comrade Hyun-gi,
Pyongyang,
25 March 2020*

---

* No one has seen or heard from Comrade Hyun-gi or his family since this date.

Acknowledgements

The Supreme Leader and the Impregnable Party extend their unwavering gratitude to the following comrades:

Comrade Williams

Comrade Signore

Comrade Issa El-Khoury

Comrade Balado

Comrade Prescott

Comrade Lord

Comrade Evans

Comrade Hillerton

Comrade Whone

Comrade Benn

Comrade Cox

Comrade Ghaffari-Parker

Comrade O'Connell

Comrade Richetti

Comrade Photiou

Comrade Short

Comrade Alexander

Oli Grant (alias Comrade Hyun-gi) was born in 1993. After graduating from the University of Bristol with a degree in English Literature and Drama, he got a job in publishing, which he is yet to be fired from. He hopes to be married with children one day.